Cl●●●●●●●●oks™

My Healthy Habits

Be Aware!
My Tips for Personal Safety

Gina Bellisario
illustrated by Renée Kurilla

Ⓜ MILLBROOK PRESS · MINNEAPOLIS

For Sofia, my lovey —G.B.

For one of my favorite brother and
sister teams, Agents K & M (Kristen
and Matt) —R.K.

Millbrook Press
A division of Lerner Publishing Group, Inc.
241 First Avenue North
Minneapolis, MN 55401 USA

For reading levels and more information, look up this title at
www.lernerbooks.com.

Main body text set in Slappy Inline 18/28.
Typeface provided by T26.

Library of Congress Cataloging-in-Publication Data

Bellisario, Gina.
    Be aware! : my tips for personal safety / by Gina Bellisario ;
    illustrated by Renée Kurilla.
      pages cm. — (Cloverleaf books. My healthy habits)
    Includes index.
    ISBN 978–1–4677–1351–1 (lib. bdg. : alk. paper)
    ISBN 978–1–4677–2537–8 (eBook)
    1. Safety education—Juvenile literature. 2. Accidents—
Prevention—Juvenile literature. 3. Crime—Prevention—Juvenile
literature. I. Kurilla, Renée, illustrator. II. Title.
HV675.5.B39 2014
613.6—dc23   2013019755

Manufactured in the United States of America
1 – BP – 12/31/13

TABLE OF CONTENTS

Chapter One

Safety Spies

Psst! I'm Agent S. That's my spy name. My real name is Sophie.

I'm on the lookout for my little brother, Will.

I help him stay safe.

Today I'm on a safety mission. Will and I are going to school. Dad wants me to look after him. That means watch for **trouble**.

Keep your eyes open, Agent W.

Two eyes can spy trouble. But four or more can do a better job. The next time you go somewhere new, bring a friend. If you or your friend sees trouble, tell a grown-up together.

Chapter Two

Sneaky Danger

It's not always easy spotting danger. Cars can be sneaky. They pop out from different places.

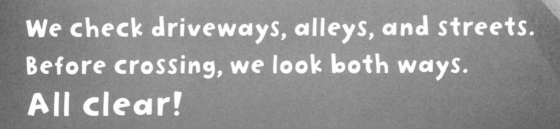

We check driveways, alleys, and streets.
Before crossing, we look both ways.
All clear!

I check street names. That way, I stay on track.

A man stops his car.

"Are you lost?" he asks.

The man seems friendly. But we don't know him.

He is a stranger.

We walk away.

Strangers can hurt you. Never go with them. If a stranger stops you, run away. Tell a trusted grown-up. Trusted grown-ups are family members. They are also people in uniform such as police officers.

Whew! I see our bus driver, Miss Olive.
Miss Olive keeps us safe on the bus.
But we lend her a hand.

We stay in our seats.

We also use quiet voices.

Going for a ride?
Stay safe in a vehicle.
Always buckle your seat
belt. And don't make loud
noises. Loud noises can
distract the driver.

Last stop: school!

We hold the handrail as we step off the bus.
Then we move out of the Danger Zone.
The Danger Zone is anywhere within 10 feet
(3 meters) of the bus.

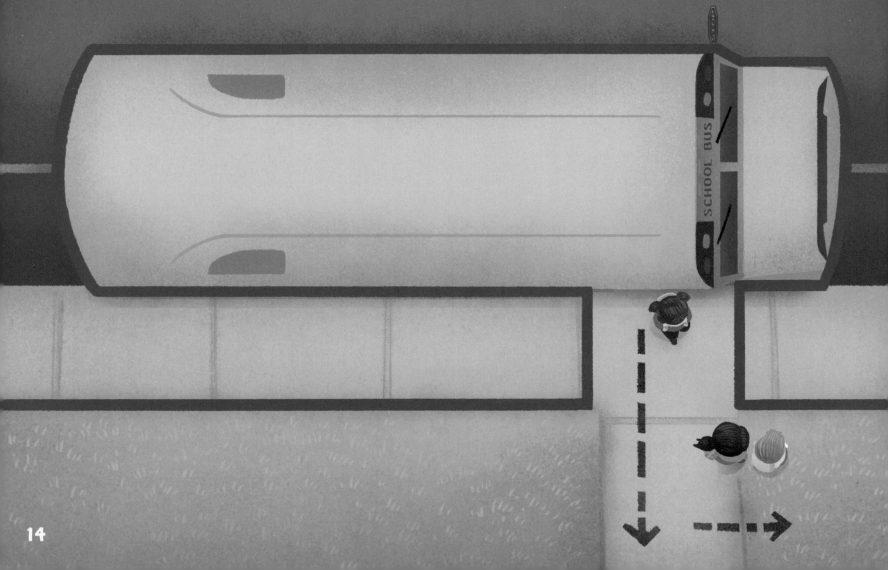

Now Miss Olive can spy us.

When you're in the Danger Zone, the bus driver may not see you. Walk into an area where you can see the driver's eyes. That's where you're the safest.

Chapter Three
Nice Work, Agent W.

In class, my spy work isn't done.
I still check up on Will.
Kids are running in the hallway.

Will makes the safe choice and walks.
He gets a **hallway safety star!**

Looks like there's **trouble** at recess.
Will wants to go down the slide.
But his classmates won't let him.

Agent W. stays calm. He tells the playground teacher. Then they solve the problem together.

Have fun the safe way. Take turns using playground equipment. And never touch broken glass or other garbage. You could catch germs or hurt yourself.

Dad picks us up after school. He says I did a good job with Will. **Mission complete!**

You can watch for trouble too.
Stay on the lookout—and stay safe!

On the Lookout

Your home is a safe place. But even the safest home has hidden dangers. Team up with your family. Find dangers that are hiding in your home. Go on the lookout!

What you need:
one or more family members
one or more pieces of paper
a pencil
a clock or a stopwatch

1) Choose a room where you will look. Will you look in the kitchen? The family room? Write the name of the room at the top of the paper.

2) For five minutes, walk around the room. Keep an eye out for things that can hurt you. When you find something that is dangerous, call out "Danger!" Make a list of what you and your family find.

3) After the five minutes are up, read the list out loud. Talk about ways to stay safe in the room. When you're done, go on the lookout in the rest of your home. Nice work, agents!

Here's a spy safety tip: Look for sharp, hot, or electrical objects. Watch for objects that can make you trip or fall too. Your home should have safety equipment, such as smoke alarms. Have a grown-up check to see if the safety equipment is working.

GLOSSARY

alleys: roads between buildings

Danger Zone: an area around the school bus where the driver may not see you. The Danger Zone is anywhere within 10 feet (3 m) of the bus.

distract: to stop someone from paying attention

handrail: a thin bar to hold for safety

mission: a job to do

smoke alarms: small devices that make a loud sound when smoke is near

uniform: a special set of clothes worn by the members of a group. Police officers, nurses, soldiers, and letter carriers wear uniforms.

BOOKS

Ajmera, Maya, Victoria Dunning, and Cynthia Pon. *Healthy Kids.* Watertown, MA: Charlesbridge, 2013.
Check out this book to see photos of kids around the world staying safe and healthy.

Bellisario, Gina. *Let's Meet a Police Officer.* Minneapolis: Millbrook Press, 2013.
Read this book to meet a community member who can help you stay safe.

Rau, Dana Meachen. *School Safety.* New York: Marshall Cavendish Benchmark, 2010.
This book explains how to make smart, safe choices in school.

WEBSITES

McGruff
http://mcgruff.org
McGruff the Crime Dog solves safety problems. Get tips for trick-or-treating, playing outside, and going online.

Safety Kids
http://www.safetykids.org
If you see a stranger, what should you do? Take a coloring book quiz and find out!

Stop Bullying
http://www.stopbullying.gov/kids/index.html
This website is from the United States Department of Health and Human Services. Meet KB, Josh, and Milton, and learn how they stand up to bullying.

LERNER ⅇ SOURCE™
Expand learning beyond the printed book. Download free, complementary educational resources for this book from our website, www.lerneresource.com.